UNDERSTANDING THE REALM
OF THE HOLY SPIRIT

Solomon Hailu, Ph.D.

Table of Content

THE NATURAL REALM

A realm is the environment in which someone, a person or some other being asserts its dominion and influence. Therefore, it is an environment controlled by a powerful entity in order to serve its interests. We may classify a realm to two areas. The first is the natural or physical realm. The second is the supernatural or spiritual realm. The natural realm refers to the physical world which is examined by our physical senses and intellect. Our physical senses are hearing, tasting, touching, smelling and seeing. We interact with the natural realm using our physical senses. The natural realm is governed by natural laws.

Our intellectual abilities involve understanding the natural realm through methods which include empirical research and data analysis to examine its existence and operations. Our natural ability may take us to the Moon and Mars but it cannot take us to Heaven. Science discovers the natural ream, it does not create it. God creates the natural realm, He does not discover it. Intellectual abilities help us to understand the natural realm which may be examined beyond our physical senses. Scientific discoveries and technological innovations enable us to better understand the natural realm and to have greater benefit from it. Technology has a growing impact upon our lives. For example, Artificial Intelligence (AI) is replacing human labor in many professions at an alarming rate. We depend on the internet for our basic services such as employment, consumer goods, health care and educational services.

The realm of the Spirit can neither be examined nor explained through scientific methods or academic studies. Science has a naturalistic view not a spiritual view. Science functions in the natural realm, not in the spiritual realm. Scientific methods can help us to better understand the natural realm which can be examined through our mere physical senses. For example, we are not able to detect the presence of germs in our body or on the surface of an object. But, we can examine the presence of germs through scientific examination using a microscope.

Science is looking for natural evidence to prove supernatural reality. However, such scientific attempts to understand and explain spiritual realities through natural observation is simply incongruous and totally insufficient. Science fails to recognize the fact that spiritual realities can only be understood by the Spirit of God. Spiritual realities can neither be detected nor analyzed through scientific thoughts or philosophical reasoning. Unsurprisingly, science denies the existence of the spiritual realm altogether as a result of its own inability to understand spiritual realities.

Despite science's unjustifiable denial of the existence of God - without a single scientific scrap of evidence – many in secular society are trapped by its ignorance of spiritual realities. They are of the view that if science cannot have an answer to their problems, there is no solution. Therefore, science has only disconnected them from seeking God and His solution to their problems. This is what is referred to in the Bible as "science falsely so called" (1 Timothy 6:26, KJV).

The natural realm also functions in the cultural, political and economic systems which have evolved through extended human interactions. For example, our cultural lifestyles such as traditions of food, religion, clothing and music have developed over long periods of time. Every one of us has been born into the realm of some culture. As children, we were raised by parents who desired to raise us in the culture they grew up with. Cultural values have played a central role in the formation of our thoughts, judgments, worldviews and overall social relationships with others. This implies that all of our activities are judged through the realm of the cultural realities of our society.

Culture is not something we can change overnight. Someone may relocate to a new country but remains in the realm of his/her old culture in the new country. For example, even though I am a naturalized United States citizen, I still exhibit much of the cultural tradition of the country of my birth. I still hold to some of the traditional cultural practices I grew up with. I even worship the Lord in a different cultural style and expression from the way people in my new country worship.

Earthly systems of politics and governments operate within the natural realm, be it a democracy or a dictatorship. All political systems function within the natural realm. All earthly governments are subject to the natural realm. Democratic systems of politics may be a good manmade system but it still functions within the natural realm. In a democracy, the government and citizens are expected to exercise their rights and responsibilities within the realm of the Constitution of the land. The Constitution stands as the supreme document governing the political, legal and bureaucratic affairs of the country. No action in that country can be expected to contradict the Constitution.

The governments in Muslim countries expect their citizens to conduct their lives in the realm of the religion of Islam. Islam has more than a religious role in the life of Muslims. Islam extends its realm into every aspect of the Muslim life. Islam is involved in social, political, cultural and economic lives of

Muslims. For example, the Islamic scriptures and teachings have established the standard norms of how Muslims should dress, the food they eat, for marriage ceremonies and family relationships as well as how to handle money and run their business. Hence, all of their actions have to be done in accordance with the prescriptions of the realm of Islamic religion.

Socialist states rule their citizens within the ideological realm of socialism which promotes collective ownership of the state under a single party rule. Socialist countries formulate their domestic and foreign policies in light of the realm of the socialist ideology. Under authoritarian rule, political, social and economic decisions can be made by the personal interests and ambitions of the ruler. A dictator wants to impose his interests upon every aspect of life in his country.

THE REALM OF THE FLESH

The realm of the flesh is where the flesh controls and influences our thoughts and actions. The passions and desires of the flesh are selfishly served. "Those who live according to the flesh have their minds set on what the flesh desires" (Romans 8:5).

The flesh is unspiritual. It is made up of earthly material. Flesh was formed from the dust of the ground (Genesis 2:7). Therefore, the flesh operates in the natural realm. The flesh interacts with the natural world through its physical senses. The flesh does not have the ability to understand spiritual things (Romans 7:15). This is to say that the flesh does not understand spiritual things because it lacks the proper tools to understand them. "The natural man does not receive the things of the Spirit of God, for they are foolishness to him; nor can he know them, because they are spiritually discerned" (1 Corinthians 2:14).

Since our flesh originated from earth, its passions and desires are earthly. The flesh does not have spiritual desires. It is not interested in heavenly revelation. It does not want to pray or fast unless made to do so. It does not desire to spend time reading the Bible. The flesh neither desires God nor desires to serve Him. Our flesh is not interested in keeping the law of God. "The mind governed by the flesh is hostile to God; for it does not submit to God's law, nor can it do so. Those who are in the realm of the flesh cannot please God" (Romans 8:7).

The flesh will eventually go back to the dust it came from. Flesh and blood cannot inherit the kingdom of God (1 Corinthians 15:50). Then, why should the flesh care about pleasing God when it eventually ends up going back to dust.

Flesh wants to find its pleasure in eating and drinking and in other pleasurable activities. The lusts of the flesh are ungodly. "The passions of the flesh are sinful" (Romans 7:5). The realm of the flesh subjects us to the realm of sin. In other words, when we live in the realm of the flesh, we live in sin.

Humanity has lived in the realm of sin since the fall of Adam. Adam was holy both in spirit and body before his fall. He was in perfect relationship with God before sin interrupted his relationship with God. But Adam was subjected to spiritual and physical death after he committed sin. God told Adam when you eat from it you will certainly die (Genesis 2:17). Adam lost his right-standing with God the moment he committed sin. Therefore, as soon as Adam committed sin, he was removed from the realm of God. So the Lord God banished him from the Garden of Eden (Genesis 3:23). Adam's act of the flesh subjected him to the realm of the devil. "The one who lives sinfully is of the devil, because the devil has been sinning since the beginning" (1 John 3:8). Adam accepted the devil's offer to commit sin which effectively discontinued his presence in God's realm (Genesis 3:6). Thereafter, Adam gave the devil legitimate authority over him and his descendants when he willingly committed sin. Adam's sinful act transferred him from the kingdom of God to the kingdom of the devil. Adam and Eve continued to live in the realm of the devil for their remaining years of life. Adam and his family suffered pain in the realm of the devil. "The Lord said Eve would suffer pain in child birth" (Genesis 3:16). "The Lord told Adam that he would suffer pain from the thorns" (Genesis 3:18). In the realm of the devil, Adam and his family suffered violence; a brother killed his own brother. "Cain attacked his brother Abel and killed him" (Genesis 4:8). For the first time, Adam suffered emotional pain and insecurity, fear, shame and nakedness. The Bible says, "they hid among the trees in the garden. The Lord God called to the man and said, "Where are you?" The man said, "I heard you walking in the garden, and I was afraid. I was naked, so I hid" (Genesis 3:9-10). Jesus declared that "the devil comes only to steal and kill and destroy" (John 10:10). The devil has continued to subject those who are not willing to renounce their sin to his realm of destruction to the present day. One cannot live in the realm of God and the realm of the devil simultaneously. The realm of God and the realm of devil never overlap with each other. We cannot have one foot in the realm of God and the other in the realm of the devil. Paul asked, "what fellowship can light have with darkness? (2 Corinthians 6:14). To live in the realm of the flesh is to live in the realm of the devil, which is the realm of sin, death and darkness. To live in the realm of God is to live in the realm of the Holy Spirit, which is God's divine realm of love, joy, peace and life. Therefore, one has to choose to live either in the realm of God or to live in the realm of the devil. Paul warned all of us that, we have an obligation—but it is not to the flesh, to live according to it. For if you live according to the flesh, you will die; but if by the Spirit you put to death the misdeeds of the body you will live (Romans 8:12-13).

Our flesh wants to continue with its sinful desires even after we are born-again. Paul admits his own personal struggle with fleshly desires when he cried out, "what a wretched man I am! Who will rescue me from this body that is subject to death?" (Romans 7:24). But he kept his flesh in check. He said, "keep control of my body, and bring it into subjection" (1

Corinthians 9:27). Paul also shares God's part in dealing with our flesh. Paul tells us that God crucified the flesh and its desires on the cross with Jesus. Paul said, "those who belong to Christ Jesus have crucified the flesh with its passions and desires" (Galatians 5:24). Therefore, sin is no longer a barrier to the realm of the Spirit for those who have died to sin. Paul said, "We are those who have died to sin" (Romans 6:2).

Paul further reminds us that "our old self was crucified with him so that the body ruled by sin might be done away with, that we should no longer be slaves to sin— because anyone who has died has been set free from sin" (Romans 6:6-7). "In the same way, count yourselves dead to sin but alive to God in Christ Jesus. Therefore, do not let sin reign in your mortal body so that you obey its evil desires. Do not offer any part of yourself to sin as an instrument of wickedness, but rather offer yourselves to God as those who have been brought from death to life; and offer every part of yourself to him as an instrument of righteousness" (Romans 6:11-13).

However, one must be willing to sacrifice the flesh. As Paul beseeches, "Therefore, I urge you, brothers and sisters, in view of God's mercy, to offer your bodies as a living sacrifice, holy and pleasing to God—this is your true and proper worship" (Romans 12:1). We need to sacrifice our body. Fire doesn't fall on empty alters. Tommy Tenney said, "If you want the fire of God, you must become the fuel of God." There has to be a sacrifice on the altar for the fire to fall. Elijah placed meat on the alter before fire came. Jesus sacrificed his body on the cross before fire came upon the disciples on the day of Pentecost. We need to sacrifice our fleshly desires to receive the fire. Crucifying the flesh will give us access to the realm of the Spirit. "If by the Spirit you put to death the misdeeds of the body, you will live" (Romans 8:13). The fact is that our death in the flesh with Christ on the cross paved the way for our new life in the realm of the Spirit. Paul declared, "I have been crucified with Christ and I no longer live, but Christ lives in me. The life I now live in the body, I live by faith in the Son of God, who loved me and gave himself for me" (Galatians 2:20). Paul teaches that since our flesh died on the cross with Christ, our flesh can no longer be a factory for sin and servant of the devil. We know that Christ has restored the lost realm of God back to our lives when he defeated sin, our flesh, death and the devil on the cross.

THE SUPERNATURAL REALM

The supernatural realm is spiritual. Only spiritual beings understand and operate in the supernatural realm. God is a Spirit being who fully understands and operates within the spiritual realm. God created other spirit beings which include angels, demons and humans. "Angels are spirits" (Hebrews 1:7). There are two groups of angels. The first are the holy angels. The holy angels are servants of God. They are involved in worship, spiritual warfare, guarding the people of God and are messengers of God. The second group of angels are the fallen angels. The devil is the master of the fallen angels. Demons are spirit beings. Jesus often referred to them as evil or unclean spirits. Demons work under the authority of Satan.

There are two states of human spirit. The first is the fallen state. This is the spirit of the natural man who is "dead" due to the sinful act of Adam. God told Adam, "when you eat from the tree you will certainly die" (Genesis 2:17). However, Adam did not immediately die in the flesh after he ate of the tree.

But his spirit immediately died at the very time he disobeyed God.

Since the fall of Adam, the spirit of the natural man could not understand the spiritual realm at all. The spirit of the natural man lost relationship with God. Therefore, the spirit of the natural man is senseless to the spiritual realm because it is dead. The spirit of the natural man does not function in the spiritual realm! "The natural man does not receive the things of the Spirit of God, for they are foolishness to him; nor can he know them, because they are spiritually discerned" (1 Corinthians 2:14).

The other state of man's spirit is when he is regenerated or born-again. The dead spirit of the natural man has to be resurrected by the life-giving Spirit of God. Jesus said, "the Spirit gives birth to spirit" (John 3:6). A born-again spirit is spiritually alive and active. It understands and operates in God's spiritual realm.

Overall, created spirit beings have a limited understanding of the spiritual realm because they are created beings. God created them with limited ability to access and operate in the spiritual realm. God has full knowledge of the character of spirit beings. However, the spirit beings do not have full knowledge of the character of God. God is beyond their comprehension. They know Him as much as He allows them to.

God created the spirit beings with a free will. That means they have the right to make choices. God does not control their decisions. God does not impose His will upon them. The spirit beings can choose whether or not to obey God. But He makes them accountable for the decisions they make and actions they take.

The spiritual realm cannot be understood by one's intellectual mind. Our intellectual mind is part of our natural mind and is guided by the physical senses. Our intellectual mind cannot understand the spiritual realm because the spiritual realm is other-worldly. Jesus said, "the people of this world neither see the Holy Spirt nor knows him" (John 14:17, MSG). The spiritual realm is a reality far away from our intellectual ability to understand it. The apostle Paul could not describe in human language his encounter of the supernatural realm. He described it as, "What no eye has seen, what no ear has heard, and what no human mind has conceived" (1 Corinthians 2:9). The prophet Isaiah became speechless when he encountered the realm of the Spirit. He said, "Woe is me, for I am undone!" (Isaiah 6:5). All he could say was "wow." The Israelites trembled at the manifested realm of the supernatural. "When the people saw the thunder and lightning and heard the trumpet and saw the mountain in smoking, they trembled with fear. They stayed at a distance" (Exodus 20:18). The realm of the Spirit is a terrifying sight. "The sight was so terrifying that Moses said, 'I am trembling with fear'" (Hebrews 12:21). I and my wife were terrified when the fire came through our roof to our living room while we were praying at 2 am. We were shaking and remained speechless for more than an hour and half.

THE REALM OF THE SPIRIT

The realm of the Spirit is the Holy Spirit's domain where he operates freely and independently. The realm of the Spirit is the Holy Spirit's dwelling place. The realm of the Spirit is in the Holy Spirit's jurisdiction. The Holy Spirit is the supreme authority in the realm of the Spirit. He exercises absolute sovereignty in the realm of the Spirit. Therefore, he has the preeminence there. The Holy Spirit demonstrates his majesty, power, glory and anointing there. He imparts his wisdom and knowledge there (Ephesians 1:17, Colossians 1:9).

The Holy Spirit has the right-of-way in the realm of the Spirit. The realm of the Spirit is the Holy Spirit's personal space and platform whereby he demonstrates his presence and power. The realm of the Spirit is a stage upon which the Holy Spirit personifies himself. Therefore, the realm of the Spirit is an embodiment of the Holy Spirit where he expresses God's love, emotion and will (Ephesians 4:30). The gifts of the Spirit operate in the realm of the Spirit (1Chrionthians 12:4-11). The Holy Spirit exhibits his fruits in the realm of the Spirit (Galatians 5:22-23).

The first thing we encounter in the realm of the Spirit is the Holy Spirit himself. When we find the Holy Spirit, we find the realm of the Spirit. The Holy Spirit is the reason for the realm of the Spirit. The Holy Spirit causes the realm of the Spirit to exist. The realm of the Spirit cannot exist apart from the Holy Spirit. The realm of the Spirit is a product of the Holy Spirit. Therefore, the Holy Spirit supersedes the realm of the Spirit as the producer is more prominent than its product. If we want to experience the realm of the Spirit, we have to allow the Holy Spirit to reign in our heart. The Holy Spirit must dwell in us before the realm of the Spirit dwells in us. Therefore, we ought to pursue the Holy Spirit himself to experience the realm of the Spirit. We cannot have access to the realm of the Spirit unless we encounter the Holy Spirit. The Holy Spirit is the reason for the existence of the realm of the Spirit. The realm of the Spirit cannot be brought into existence by any other means. No human intellect or religious rituals can create the realm of the Spirit. We must encounter the Holy Spirit to have his realm in us. Jesus told his disciples to receive the Holy Spirit (Acts 1:4-5). Jesus emphasized that we must build a relationship with the Holy Spirit. We must allow him to dwell in us. The Holy Spirit transforms our thoughts and opinions after he establishes his realm in us.

The Holy Spirit wants to indwell our life and establish his realm in us. Without allowing the Holy Spirit to come into our lives, we will not allow his realm to guide us. In other words, unless the Holy Spirit lives in us, we do not qualify to move in the realm of the Spirit. The Holy Spirit wants to bring his realm into us in order to bring his blessing into us. Therefore, we must make ourselves available to the Holy Spirit to serve as a platform for his realm.

The realm of the Spirit can be illustrated as a breadbasket of a baker. The baker owns the breadbasket and uses it for a specific purpose, either to hold the bread or to carry it. The realm of the Spirit plays a similar role as a breadbasket. It hosts the presence of the Holy Spirit. The Holy Spirit builds the realm of the Spirit to primarily host his presence and serve his purpose. Paul said, "You are in the realm of the Spirit, if indeed the Spirit of God lives in you" (Romans 8:9). Paul further notes that "the person without the Spirit does not accept the things that come from the Spirit of God but considers them foolishness and cannot understand them because they are discerned only through the Spirit" (1 Corinthians 2:14). We cannot experience the realm of the Spirit without the Holy Spirit.

The realm of the Spirit exists to serve the exclusive will and purpose of the Holy Spirit. The realm of the Spirit has no reason to exist except to serve the will and purpose of the Holy Spirit. The Holy Spirit prepares his realm to strictly serve his will, not to serve the will of man. The Holy Spirit reveals his mind (knowledge) in the realm of the Spirit. Our mind cannot understand the mind of the Holy Spirit unless we have him to form his realm in us. "Those who live in accordance with the Spirit have their minds set on what the Spirit desires" (Acts 8: 6). The

Holy Spirit has his influence upon our mind after establishing his realm in us.

However, the Holy Spirit does not force his realm upon anybody. We have to be willing to receive the Holy Spirit and continue to allow him to dwell in us to maintain his realm in our lives. If we deny the Holy Spirit access to our lives, we deny the realm of the Spirit to guide our lives. The Holy Spirit expects us to open our hearts to him. We get exposed to the thoughts of the Spirit in the realm of the Spirit. The Holy Spirit reveals his mind in the realm of the Spirit.

FORMATION OF THE REALM OF THE SPIRIT

The Holy Spirit does not have a static physical body. He is Spirit. Therefore, he uses physical objects, symbols and images to demonstrate his presence and power. The Bible tells us that the Holy Spirit manifests his realm through different physical objects such us the Ark of the Covenant, Solomon's temple, water, rain, river, fire, light, blood, oil, cloud, smoke, wind, mountains, rock, dust, bread, plants, animal such as the donkey, dove or the human body and their belongings such as Jesus' clothes, Paul's handkerchief, Peter's shadow, Moses's rod and Elisha's rod.

The realm of the Spirit becomes evident to us the moment the Holy Spirit uses the natural object he chooses. The Holy Spirit manifests his realm for a specific purpose. It is up to the Holy Spirit to decide which object to use, when, for how long and for what purpose. Some men and women of God have usurped the realm of the Spirit for many decades, while the realm of the Sprit did not last longer in others' lives.

The physical objects used by the Holy Spirit are not the actual person of the Holy Spirit. They are the physical instruments the Holy Spirit uses to extend his realm. The Holy Spirit often finds a physical object to work through. The object serves as host for the Holy Spirit to demonstrate his work through.

The Holy Spirit may establish his realm upon the natural objects anywhere in the universe without asking for permission from anybody. No natural power can prevent him to form his realm wherever he wants. The prophet Isaiah asked, "Who has directed the Spirit of the Lord, or as His counselor has taught Him?" (Isaiah 40:13).

The Holy Spirit moves with unstoppable power. Jesus presented the Holy Spirit as rivers (John 7:38). Rivers can make their way to any direction they want to go. They have cut through rocks, beautiful terrain and rugged places for thousands of years. The Holy Spirit came upon the disciples on the day of Pentecost as an unstoppable violent wind. "Suddenly a sound like the blowing of a violent wind came from heaven and filled the whole house where they were sitting" (Acts 2:2). No other natural force can stop the move of the wind. "No one has power over the wind to contain it" (Ecclesiastes 8:8). Jesus said, "The wind goes wherever it wants to go. The wind blows wherever it pleases. You hear its sound, but you cannot tell where it comes from or where it is going" (John 3:8).

The Holy Spirit manifested himself as fire on the day of Pentecost. "They saw what seemed to be tongues of fire that separated and came to rest upon each of them" (Acts 2:3). Fire is an unstoppable natural force. No one can guide fire where to go. Fire does not need direction from anybody. It consumes everything it finds on the way to its destiny.

The scripture presents the Holy Spirit as rain which is another unstoppable natural force. "Be glad, people of Zion, rejoice in the Lord your God, for he has given you the autumn rains because he is faithful. He sends you abundant showers, both autumn and spring rains, as before" (Joel 2:23). The rain does not come at man's will or power. The weather man can only report its approach. Nobody is left out when the rain comes to the area. The Holy Spirit is like unstoppable rain. He can pour out as much of himself as he wants. The Holy Spirit poured upon all of the disciples like a rain on the day of Pentecost. Peter said, "The Holy Spirit was poured upon all people" (Acts 2:17, 33).

The Holy Spirit also appeared as an unstoppable cloud. Cloud is another unstoppable natural force. It can cover the entire area. No one can get rid of it. For example, "the priests could not continue their temple service when the cloud, for the glorious presence of the Lord filled the Temple of God" (2 Chronicles 5:14). Moses entered a cloud as he went on up the mountain. "There he stayed fo forty days and forty nights" (Exodus 24:18). A cloud covered Jesus and his disciples on the mountain of transfiguration. "While he was speaking, a cloud appeared and covered them, and they were afraid as they entered the cloud" (Luke 9:34).

The Holy Spirt also appeared as a bright light to lead the children of Israel. "By day the Lord went ahead of them in a pillar of cloud to guide them on their way and by night in a pillar of fire to give them light, so that they could travel by day or night" (Exodus 13:21). The Spirit of God was shining upon the face of Moses. "When Moses came down from Mount Sinai with the two tablets of the covenant law in his hands, he was not aware that his face was radiant because he had spoken with the Lord. When Aaron and all the Israelites saw Moses, his face was radiant, and they were afraid to come near him" (Exodus 34:29-30).

The Holy Spirit revealed himself in those powerful natural ways to show that he is an unstoppable powerful entity. The Psalmist said, "Where can I go from your Spirit? Where can I flee from your presence? If I go up to the heavens, you are there; if I make my bed in the depths, you are there" (Psalm 139:7-8).

The Holy Spirit can form his realm free from physical conditions or natural circumstances. For example, the Holy Spirit extended his realm upon the earth while it was formless, empty, and covered with darkness (Genesis 1:2). The Holy Spirit set up his realm on earth for the first time in precreation. The Holy Spirit was on earth before there was life on earth. Prior to the activity of the Holy Spirit, the earth was lifeless, formless, empty and covered with darkness. The earth's environment was not prepared to host life. The Holy Spirit had to prepare it to host life. "When you send your Spirit, they are created, and you renew the face of the ground" (Psalms 104:30).

However, the first thing the Holy Spirit did on earth was to establish his realm upon it. For that purpose, the Holy Spirit searched for an object to rest his realm upon. Water was a natural object the Holy Spirit used to extend his realm on earth. The Bible tells us that the Spirit of God was hovering over the face of the waters (Genesis 1:2). The Holy Spirit used waters as a point of contact to extend the realm of the Spirit upon the entire earth. Once the Holy Spirit established his realm over the water, he began his creative work. The Bible tells us that the earth was formed out of water and by water (2 Peter 3:5). All life on the earth has had to depend on water since creation. Plants and animals are sustained by water.

The Holy Spirit arrived on the waters before God established His kingdom on earth at the garden of Eden. Before the kingdom of God was established on earth, the Holy Spirit formed his realm over the waters. The Holy Spirit came to earth not just to make a way for God to begin His creation work on earth. God sent His Spirit to earth to make a way for the establishment of the Kingdom of God on earth. Therefore, the kingdom of God was established upon the realm of the Holy Spirit. The Holy Spirit had no greater mission than to establish the kingdom of God upon earth.

The Holy Spirit's act of establishing the realm of the Spirit on the water made the way for Father God to start His creation work on earth. God sent His words to earth for the first time after the Holy Spirit established his realm upon the surface of the water. God spoke His Word to the water itself. God said, "Let there be a vault between the waters to separate water from water" (Genesis 1:6). God and the Holy

Spirit continued the joint venture of their creation work on earth in the realm of the Holy Spirit. As the Holy Spirit expanded his realm on earth, God also continued to speak until He populated the earth with life. Genesis 1-14 says that God repeatedly spoke to create life on earth by declaring "let there be or let it be..."

In the realm of the Spirit, mankind and all other creations came into existence. God's creation enjoyed the goodness of God. "God saw all that he had made, and it was very good" (Genesis 1:31). Life in the realm of the Spirit was good. Man was able to hear the voice of God on a daily basis in the continuous presence of the realm of the Spirit on earth. Adam enjoyed a good life in the realm of the Spirit until his fall. The last time Adam heard the voice of God was in Genesis 3:8-9, which reads, "then the man and his wife heard the Lord God as he was walking in the garden in the cool of the day, and they hid from the Lord God among the trees of the garden. Adam subjected himself to the realm of Satan from that day on. The realm of Satan was characterized as being filled with pain, murder, hate, weakness, division, sin and death. Man knew none of those tragedies while he was in the realm of God in the Garden.

However, the Holy Spirit continued to establish his realm upon natural objects albeit in a limited way. In the Old Testament, the Holy Spirit has extended his realm upon the chosen servants of the Lord with the exception that the Spirit of the Lord entered the prophet Ezekiel to do special temporary assignment. The Prophet Ezekiel said, "the Spirit came into me and raised me to my feet, and I heard him speaking to me" (Ezekiel 2:2). Again, Ezekiel said, "The Spirit of God then entered me and made me stand on my feet, and He spoke with me" (Ezekiel 3:24). However, the Holy Spirit came upon all the other Old Testament servants of God during the Old Testament including, the Patriarchs, Priests, Kings and Prophets. For example, Noah was in the realm of the Spirit when he built the Ark for God. The so-called Patriarchs (Abraham, Isaac and Jacob) and Joseph walked with God in the realm of the Spirit.

Moses entered the realm of the Holy Spirit at the burning bush. The Holy Spirit set up his realm upon the burning bush. Moses was in the natural realm before the Holy Spirit charged the environment with his realm. He was immediately instructed to remove his sandals to enter into the realm of the Spirit (Exodus 3:5). God asked him to remove his Egyptian wisdom and his personal strength. Moses did not deliver Israel by the realm of his Egyptian wisdom nor with his Jewish identity but by the realm of the Holy Spirit. Therefore, the first thing God did to Moses was to move him from his natural realm to the realm of the Spirit.

After he entered the realm of the Spirit, Moses was able to hear the voice of God for the first time. God called him from within the bush, "Moses! Moses!" And Moses said, "Here I am" (Exodus 3:4-9). The realm of the Spirit also paved the way for Moses to experience signs and wonders (Exodus 4:2-3). As Moses continued to be in the realm of the Spirit, his experience of encountering the powerful delivering hand of God continued to grow to a higher dimension. He brought judgment on the Egyptians in the realm of the Spirit. He divided the Red Sea in the realm of the Spirit. He ruled over the Israelites for forty years under the realm of the Spirit.

Samson was another example of a person who acted in the realm of the Spirit for about twenty years. The Bible tells us that the Spirit of God used to come upon Samson to enable him to act in the realm of the Spirit. The Spirit of the Lord came upon Samson with power. "Samson tore the lion apart like one tears a young goat. He had nothing in his hand (Judges 14:6). However, Samson could no longer operate within the realm of the Spirit after the Lord had left him" (Judges 16:20). His loss of the Holy Spirt from his life caused Samson to have a tragic ending.

Another Bible figure is King Saul. Saul began his kingship after the Holy Spirit came upon him (1 Samuel 10:1). However, after forty years as a king of Israel, the Holy Spirit left him, and he could no longer act within the realm of the Spirit" (1 Samuel 18:10). King David was another person who powerfully encountered the Spirit of the Lord. He was willing to receive the Holy Spirit into his life when the prophet Samuel was asked to anoint him to become the next king of Israel. "The prophet Samuel took the horn of oil and anointed him in the presence of his brothers, and from that day on, the Spirit of the Lord came powerfully upon David" (1 Samuel 1:13). King David pleaded with God not to take His Spirit away from him (Psalm 51:11). He sought the Spirit not the realm of the Spirit. David knew that the Spirit of the Lord was the source of the realm of the Spirit throughout his life. He first encountered the Spirit, then the realm of the Spirit followed. After the Holy Spirit came upon him, he automatically came under the realm of the Spirit. David could do impossible things in the realm of the Spirit. For example, he defeated Goliath in the realm of the Spirit. He ruled Israel for forty years in the realm of the Spirit. He wrote his psalms in the realm of the Spirit.

THE INDWELLING OF THE HOLY SPIRIT

In the New Testament, the Holy Spirit dwells inside the born-gain believers. The Apostle Paul said to the Corinthian believers, "you are a temple of God and that the Spirit of God dwells in you" (1 Corinthians 3:16). The greatest honor God bestowed upon a born-again believer is to be a temple of the Holy Spirit. Nothing is more prominent than being the dwelling place of the Holy Spirit. Being the host of the Holy Spirit is a greater honor than receiving physical healing. Being the host of the Holy Spirit is more honorable than serving God with the gift of the working of miracles. Being the temple of the Holy Spirit is more honorable than holding ministry titles. To be born-again has greater benefit than speaking in other tongues or operating in other gifts of the Spirit. Being the dwelling place of the Holy Spirit gives believes the greatest privilege to have the presence of the Almighty Spirit of God in their lives. What can be a greater honor than having the Holy Spirit dwell in one's life?

Being born-again from the Holy Spirit establishes an eternal bond with the Holy Spirit. A born-again believer has eternal fellowship with the Holy Spirit. Other manifestations of the Holy Spirit, be it performing miracles, speaking in tongues, prophesying or receiving anointing for ministry are temporary engagements with the Holy Spirit as those experiences will go away.

The Holy Spirit waits for the invitation to dwell in one's life. He does not force his way into a person's life to get him born-again. If the person does not allow the Holy Spirit to come, he will not enter his life. The Holy Spirit enters a life of a person when that person sincerely repents of his/her sins. Repentance invites the Holy Spirit into a person's life. Peter said, "Repent and be baptized, every one of you, in the name of Jesus Christ for the forgiveness of your sins. And you will receive the gift of the Holy Spirit" (Acts 2:38).

Repentance is not just getting rid of our sins. It is the bedrock for the Holy Spirit in our lives. No other power can bring the Holy Spirit into the believer's life except one's willingness to repent. A genuinely repentant person becomes the dwelling place of the Holy Spirit. Repentance is not just receiving forgiveness from God, it is the only way for the Holy Spirit to extend his realm into the life of a person.

The indwelling Spirit of God brings with him a number of blessings. First, the Holy Spirit gives new birth to the spirit of the born-again person. In other words, the Holy Spirit saves the spirit of the born-again believer. He saved us through the washing of rebirth and renewal by the Holy Spirit (Titus 3:5). A born-again believer is a saved person. Therefore, the biggest miracle the Holy Spirit does is salvation. No other miracle is greater than the miracle of salvation! Being saved is the greatest miracle a believer can have.

Second, the indwelling Spirit of God brings an anointing into the life of a born-again believer. A born-again person receives the anointing from the Holy Spirit the moment he is born-again. The only condition to receive the anointing is to be born-again through the Holy Spirit who is the giver of the anointing. The Holy Spirit and the anointing are inseparable. When a born-again believer receives the Holy Spirit, he will have the anointing. A born-again believer does not get anointed only when he is ordained by a church to became a minister or when he stands in the pulpit to minister. A born-again believer does not get anointed when he receives a ministry title such as Apostle, Prophet or Pastor. A born--again believer does not get anointed when he graduates from a seminary or Bible college. A born-again believer is anointed the moment the Holy Spirit indwells him. Therefore, every born-again believer is anointed. St. John tells us that you have an anointing from the Holy One (1 John 2:20). As for you, the anointing you received from him remains in you (1 John 2:27). Paul told the Christian believers God anointed us (2 Corinthians 1:21). The anointing was given to all believers. Not just for church leaders. Every born-again believer lives in the realm of the anointing.

All believers receive the same anointing Jesus and the apostles received from the Holy Spirit. "For we were all baptized by one Spirit so as to form one body—whether Jews or Gentiles, slave or free—and we were all given the one Spirit to drink (1 Corinthians 12:13). Peter said, "God accepted them (gentiles) by giving the Holy Spirit to them, just as he did to us" (Acts 15:8). There are no different kinds of anointing. Again, Peter said, "God gave them the same gift he gave us" (Acts 11:17). No one is more anointed than the other! God anointed us all with the same anointing. But there are different kinds of calling and ministries. However, we receive the same anointing to do different tasks. We may experience different levels of the work of the anointing in our ministry, depending upon how open we are for more anointing. The more we hunger for the anointing, the more the anointing is available for us. The anointing is not limited unless we limit him. We can limit our experience with the anointing based on our limited desire for him. There is no level for the anointing because it is limitless. It is beyond measure. The Holy Spirit is unlimited, but human ability to engage the Holy Spirit is limited. We have limited exercise in the anointed as a born-again believer unless we open ourselves for more. Many born-again believers ask God for a double portion of the anointing based on the prayer of Elisha for a double anointing. The Bible says, "God told Elijah to anoint Elisha" (1 Kings 19:16). God did not say to Elijah to give Elisha a double anointing. Elisha asked for a limited level of anointing which was double of the anointing upon Elijah. God gave Elisha a double anointing because he asked for it. God could have given Elisha unlimited levels of anointing had he not asked for a double anointing. Elisha limited the amount of the anointing he wanted to receive from God. Therefore, God gave him as much as he asked. However, it does not mean that God has a limited amount of anointing. Elisha asked for a double portion of anointing because he had faith to operate in a double anointing. Elisha decided the level of anointing he wanted to receive. It was neither God not Elijah who decided the level of the anointing Elisha would receive.

We are not supposed to limit ourselves with Elisha's experience with the anointing as the New Testament believers. God has unlimited anointing to give to New Testament believers. God gives the Spirit without limit (John 3:34). For example, God poured our His Spirit upon the disciples on the day of Pentecost. He did not limit his Spirit to a double portion. Therefore, we have to be open to receive the anointing from the Holy Spirit beyond measure. God gives His anointing without measure. Third, the indwelling Spirit of God saturates the spirit of the born-again believer with power. Jesus said, "you will receive power when the Holy Spirit comes on you" (Acts 1:8). A born-again believer begins to walk in the realm of power the moment he received the Holy Spirit. The realm of the Spirit is the realm of power. Jesus received power the moment he received the Holy Spirit's anointing. "God anointed Jesus of Nazareth with the Holy Spirit and power, and he went around doing good and healing all who were under the power of the devil, because God was with him" (Acts 10:38).

Jesus ministered under the mighty power of the Holy Spirit. The power of the Holy Spirit surpasses all other powers. The power of the Holy Spirit is immeasurable. No natural, spiritual or human power withstands the power of the Holy Spirit. Jesus defeated the power of the devil, diseases, death and other natural powers everywhere he went by the mighty power of the Holy Spirit. Luke said, "Jesus returned to Galilee in the power of the Spirit" (Luke 4:14). "The power of the Lord was with Jesus to heal the sick" (Luke 5:17). The people all tried to touch him, because power was coming from him and healing them all (Luke 6:19). Jesus said, "Someone touched me; I know that power has gone out from me" (Luke 8:46). "Then they were all amazed and spoke among themselves, saying, "What a word this is! For with authority and power He commands the unclean spirits, and they come out"" (Luke 4:36). The power of the Holy Spirit was present while Jesus was teaching. "People were astonished at His teaching, for His word was with power" (Luke 4:32).

The disciples received the same power Jesus received on the day of Pentecost. Jesus said to them, "you will receive power when the Holy Spirit comes upon you" (Acts 1:8). The Holy Spirit came upon them as a powerful wind (Acts 2:2). They demonstrated the power of the Holy Spirit during their ministry. Paul said, "my message and my preaching were not with wise and persuasive words, but with a demonstration of the Spirit's power" (1 Corinthians 2:4). In His letter to the Romans, the Apostle Paul said, "I will not venture to speak of anything except what Christ has accomplished through me in leading the Gentiles to obey God by what I have said and done by the power of signs and wonders, through the power of the Spirit of God. So from Jerusalem all the way around to Illyricum, I have fully proclaimed the gospel of Christ" (Romans 15:18-19). Paul further declared that "God has not given us a spirit of fear, but of power" (2 Timothy 1:7). Paul proclaimed the message of the gospel with power in the presence of political and religious leaders. For example, governor Felix was afraid and said, "That's enough for now! You may leave. When I find it convenient, I will send for you" (Acts 24:25). Peter and John proclaimed Christ in front of the

Jewish leaders with boldness and power. "When they saw the courage of Peter and John and realized that they were unschooled, ordinary men, they were astonished" (Acts 4:13).

God made the same power that worked in Jesus and his disciples available to us today. Jesus delegated the same power he had to his disciples. "Then the same great power which raised Jesus from the dead is working in us today" (Ephesians 1:19). The apostle Paul declared to the Ephesian believers, "Now to Him who is able to do exceedingly abundantly above all that we ask or think, according to the power that works in us" (Ephesians 3:20). The apostle Paul is saying that the power of God is available to us now. The same mighty power of God is working in our midst. The same mighty power is working today! God's power never stopped working with Jesus or with his disciples. Some say God is not doing miracles anymore. But that is simply not true. Our God is all the time powerful. He has delivered many from physical, spiritual and emotional affliction throughout church history. I have personally witnessed countless numbers of people delivered by the power of God from demons, diseases, depression, substance abuse and trauma in the many years of my ministry. Fourth, the indwelling Spirit of God pours the love of God into the spirit of the born-again believer (Romans 15:30). God deposits His divine love into the born-again believer through the Holy Spirt to extend His love to the world through the beliver. A born-again believer loves others the way God loves him. As God's love operates in the heart of the born-again believer, he/she begins to love others unconditionally. For example, the born-again believer loves others, not based on shared racial or ethnic identity or based on others political views or economic status. The born-again believer loves others with God's kind of love because he received God's love through the Holy Spirit who dwells in him. God's love has been poured into our hearts through the Holy Spirit who has been given to us (Romans 5:5). Fear, anxiety, depression and other emotional disorders will no longer linger in the born-again believer's heart. Paul reminds us that God has not given us a spirit of fear, but of power and of love and of a sound mind (2 Timothy 1:7). Fifth, the indwelling Spirit of God fills the heart of the born-again believer with his joy. Jesus was full of joy through the Holy Spirit (Luke 10:21). Similarly, a born-again believer experiences the joy of God through the Holy Spirit (1 Thessalonians 1:6). The disciples were filled with joy and with the Holy Spirit (Acts 13:52). A born-again believer is the most joyful person on earth due to the presence of the Holy Spirit in his life. Fear, anxiety, stress, depression have no room in the heart of the born-again believer. The born-again believer is unconditionally joyful. The apostles were joyful in the midst of persecutions. "Then they left the presence of the council, rejoicing that they were counted worthy to suffer dishonor for the name" (Acts 5:4). Six, the indwelling Spirit of God brings divine peace into the heart of a born-again believer. The Holy Spirit is the source of peace and joy (Romans 14:17). Seven, the believer receives an overflow of hope by the power of the Holy Spirit (Romans 15:13).

THE INWORKING OF THE HOLY SPIRIT

The Holy Spirit begins to transform the life of the born-again believer from the moment he/she is born-again. The first inworking of the Holy Spirit is sanctification. Sanctification is an ongoing work of the Holy Spirit to help the born-again believes to live a holy life. The Holy Spirit is Holy (Romans 1:4). The Holy Spirit is holy in character and actions. He works to implant his holiness in the heart of a born-again believer in the process of sanctification. The apostle Paul said, "You are sanctified just by the Holy Spirit" (Romans 15:16). Sanctification cannot be achieved by good deeds. Sanctification is an enduring work of the Holy Spirit that brings holiness into the life of the born-again believer. Sanctification cannot be completed with a single act of the Holy Spirit. Nor can sanctification bring complete and perfect holiness into the life of the believer in just a single moment. The believer undergoes a progressive process of change in thinking and actions during the process of sanctification. Therefore, sanctification is an ongoing work of the Holy Spirit throughout the earthly life of the born-again believer.

The Holy Spirit takes three steps in the process of sanctification. The first step is salvation. The process of sanctification begins at the moment of salvation. The apostle Paul said, "God from the beginning chose you for salvation through sanctification by the Spirit" (2 Thessalonians 2:13). Salvation is a part of the Holy Spirit's work of sanctification.

The second part is separation of the born-again believer. The Holy Spirit progressively works to set apart the believer from sinful practices of the flesh. Paul said, "by the Spirit you put to death the misdeeds of the body" (Roman 8:13). The born-again believer begins to have a change of mind towards his/her past sinful life at the moment of salvation. Paul said, "put off your old self, which belongs to your former manner of life and is corrupt through deceitful desires, and be renewed in the spirit of your minds, and put on the new self, created after the likeness of God in true righteousness and holiness" (Ephesians 4:22-23).

However, the born-again believer will continue to struggle with the flesh even though his attitude towards sin and the flesh has changed. The flesh is unredeemed. The flesh continues to relentlessly pursue its desires. It tries to distract the born-again believer from pursuing holiness at every conceivable opportunity. Nonetheless, the Holy Spirit continues to sanctify the born-again believer regularly. The Holy Spirit counters the work of the flesh in the life of a born-again believer. The Holy Spirit sets the mind of the born-again person on spiritual things. "Those who live in accordance with the Spirit have their minds set on what the Spirit desires" (Romans 8:9).

However, the believer must be willing to go through the sanctification process which requires him to deny the flesh from performing its acts through cooperation with the Holy Spirit. The Holy Spirit cannot do it alone. He needs our partnership to make his of work sanctification fruitful. Paul says, "for just as you presented your members as slaves of uncleanness, and of lawlessness leading to more lawlessness, so now present your members as slaves of righteousness for holiness" (Romans 6:19). Though sanctification cannot completely get rid of the desires of the flesh, the desires of the flesh can be tamed through the sanctification process.

The third part of sanctification is transformation of a born-again believer into the image of Christ by the Holy Spirit. "We are being transformed into his image (Christ) with ever-increasing glory, which comes from the Lord, who is the Spirit" (2 Corinthians 3:18). The Holy Spirit builds the character of Christ in the life of the born-again believer. The Character trait of Christ includes holiness, humility, kindness, gentleness, patience, self-control, loving, forgiveness, humbleness, meekness and mindfulness of others. Be completely humble and gentle; be patient, bearing with one another in love (Ephesians 4:1).

The blood of Jesus cleanses the sins the believer might commit according to 1 John 1:7-9. The blood of Jesus does not sanctify. The blood of Jesus does not change the character of the believer. The blood of Jesus only washes the believer from recurring sin. The Holy Spirit changes the character of the born-again believer to not be subject to sin but to be transformed to a Christlike character through sanctification.

The second inworking of the Holy Spirit is building the relationship between the born-again believer and God the Father. The born-again believer becomes God-conscious through the inworking of the Holy Spirit. Because of this inworking, a born-again believer desires to know God more and more. Our fellowship with the Holy Spirit leads us into fellowship with God the Father. When we have fellowship with the Holy Spirit, we have fellowship with God. We cannot have fellowship with God the Father without having fellowship with the Holy Spirit. A born-again believer's relationship with the Father is confirmed by the Holy Spirit. A born-again believer begins to learn how to converse with God. Remember that the born-again believer is just like a brand new baby who needs to grow spiritually. One does not understand everything at the baby stage, but will grow to know God. The Holy Spirit leads us into fellowship with the Father. "For those who are led by the Spirit of God are the children of God" (Romans 8:14). The Holy Spirit teaches the person to have a desire to intimately relate to his heavenly Father. We begin to call out "Abba, Father." "God sent the Spirit of His Son into our hearts, the Spirit who calls out, "Abba, Father'" (Galatians 4:6). The Holy Spirit teaches one about God. The one begins to openly seek God. He gets hungry for more of God. He wants to worship God. He begins to walk with God. "We have received, not the spirit of the world, but the Spirit who is from God, that we might know the things that have been freely given to us by God" (I Corinthians 2:12).

The third inworking of the Holy Spirit is leading the born-again believer to engage in the true worship of God. To worship God is to revere or adore God. The true worshiper worship God with the help of the Holy Spirit. The Holy Spirit is the Spirit of truth. Jesus said, "When the Spirit of truth, comes, he will guide you into all the truth" (John 16:13). A true worship is not an act of the flesh or an act of offering certain religious rituals. God is not impressed with such acts of worship. True worship is not a physical act, but a spiritual act. True worship must come from the spirit of the worshipper. The Holy Spirit inspires the spirit of the believer to worship God. One must be born-again through the Holy Spirit to become a true worshipper. A born-again believer who has the dwelling of the Spirit begins to worship God in truth. The Holy Spirit is a true worshipper. Our worship is accepted by God when the Holy Spirit is our worship leader. Our worship impresses God when the Holy Spirit leads our worship. The Holy Spirit is the best worshipper of God because he truly knows God the most. The Holy Spirit is fascinated by God the Father more than anything else. True worship is inspired by the Holy Spirit. Jesus said, "A time is coming and has now come when the true worshipers will worship the Father in the Spirit and in truth, for they are the kind of worshipers the Father seeks. God is spirit, and his worshipers must worship in the Spirit and in truth" (John 4:24). True worship moves God. For example,

"In the year that King Uzziah died, I saw the Lord, high and exalted, seated on a throne; and the train of his robe filled the temple. Above him were seraphim, each with six wings: With two wings they covered their faces, with two they covered their feet, and with two they were flying. And they were calling to one another: 'Holy, holy, holy is the Lord Almighty; the whole earth is full of his glory.' At the sound of their voices the doorposts and thresholds shook and the temple was filled with smoke" (Isaiah 6:1-4). No other power moves God like true worship. Prayer brings God's blessings into our lives, whereas, true worship brings God into our lives.

True worship brings the very presence of God. "The trumpeters and musicians joined in unison to give praise and thanks to the Lord. Accompanied by trumpets, cymbals and other instruments, the singers raised their voices in praise to the Lord and sang: 'He is good; his love endures forever.'" "Then the temple of the Lord was filled with the cloud, and the priests could not perform their service because of the cloud, for the glory of the LORD filled the temple of God" (2 Chronicles 5:14).

True worship brings revelation. "Now bring me a harpist. While the harpist was playing, the hand of the Lord came on Elisha and he said, "This is what the Lord says: I will fill this valley with pools of water. For this is what the Lord says: You will see neither wind nor rain, yet this valley will be filled with water, and you, your cattle and your other animals will drink" (2 Kings 3:15-17).

True worship brings deliverance. "About midnight Paul and Silas were praying and singing hymns to God, and the other prisoners were listening to them. Suddenly there was such a violent earthquake that the foundations of the prison were shaken. At once all the prison doors flew open, and everyone's chains came loose" (Acts 16:25-26).

True worship brings healing. And behold, a leper came and worshiped Him, saying, "Lord, if You are willing, You can make me clean" (Matthew 8:2).

The fourth inworking of the Holy Spirit forms a bond between the born-again believer and Christ. John 14:26 reminds us: "But the Helper, the Holy Spirit, whom the Father will send in My name, He will teach you all things, and bring to your remembrance all that I said to you." The Holy Spirit helps us to follow Christ on daily basis. Jesus said, "When the Advocate comes, whom I will send to you from the Father—the Spirit of truth who goes out from the Father—he will testify about me" (John 15:26-27). A born-again believer is well-positioned to receive revelations from Christ through the Holy Spirit. A born-again believer begins to reflect the very life of Christ.

The fifth inworking of the Holy Spirit is to help believer to forgive others. The believer receives a special grace from the Holy Spirit to forgive those who did wrong to them. Jesus breathed on them and said, "Receive the Holy Spirit. If you forgive anyone's sins, their sins are forgiven; if you do not forgive them, they are not forgiven" (John 20:22-23). Jesus gave them the Holy Spirit before he instructed them to forgive others. He gave them the ability to forgive through the Holy Spirit. The born-again believer cannot harbor offenses in his heart because the Holy Spirit is in him. The believer receives the help he needs from the Holy Spirit to forgive those who have offended him. No one who has received the Holy Spirit is unable to forgive the sin of others unless he decides not to forgive others. It has to be noted that when we are not willing to forgive others of their sins, we are bearing a burden of sin in our own lives. Jesus said, "If you do not forgive others their sins, your Father will not forgive your sins" (Matthew 6:15). We need to be willing to cooperate with the Holy Spirit who is in our lives to help us truly forgive others. Forgiveness is not a choice, it is an obligation. Forgiveness imparts spiritual, physical, emotional and social benefit to us. Spiritually, forgiveness helps us to keep a good relationship with the Holy Spirit. If we do not forgive others, we grieve the Holy Spirit. We cannot afford to have unforgiveness spoil our relationship with the Holy Spirit. We grieve the Holy Spirit when we are not forgiving other (Ephesians 4:31). Unforgiveness also spoils our relationship with the Father. Jesus said, "but if you do not forgive others their sins, your Father will not forgive your sins" (Mathew 6:15). Forgiveness sets a stage for good emotions in our lives. Our heart will be filled with sense of joy, peace and happiness after we forgive others.

Forgiveness also helps to improve our physical health and wellness. Forgiveness provides many health benefits to our mind and body as does regular physical exercise. Scientific studies show that a person who forgives lives healthier life. Among other things, forgiveness can lead to healthier relationships, improved mental health, less anxiety, stress and hostility, fewer symptoms of depression, lower blood pressure, a stronger immune system, improved heart health and improved self-esteem. Socially, forgiveness helps to keep good friendship with others. Having good friendship is one of the essentials elements of healthy lifestyle. The Bible says, "Make every effort to live in peace with everyone" (Hebrews 12:14).

Six, the believer receives spiritual gifts from the indwelling Spirit of God. "For to one is given the word of wisdom through the Spirit, to another the word of knowledge through the same Spirit, to another faith by the same Spirit, to another gifts of healing by the same Spirit, to another the working of miracles, to another prophecy, to another discerning of spirits, to another different kinds of tongues, to another the interpretation of tongues" (1 Corinthians 12:8-11). Some of these gifts mature in the life of the new believer as his relationship with the Holy Spirit grows.

Seventh, the believer walks in liberty because of the indwelling of the Spirit. The Spirit of the Lord brings liberty to the life of the believer. "Now the Lord is the Spirit, and where the Spirit of the Lord is, there is freedom" (2 Corinthians 3:17). The Holy Spirit gives us power over the works of darkness. No stronghold remains powerful after the Holy Spirit takes charge of the life of the believer. The moment the Holy Spirit dwells in us, fear, anxiety, depression and emotional related stresses disappear. Jesus referred to the Holy Spirit as "the Comforter" (John 16:7). The born-again believer gets delivered from sin and its consequences such as physical, mental and emotional sickness. I was delivered from an incurable condition the moment I was born-again. A born-again person may get delivered from powerful addictions, religious spirits, generational curses, compulsive sins and demonic operations the moment the Spirit of God gives the person the newly-born status. He destroys every stronghold in the life of a person being born again. A believer is no longer under the realm of Satan. Every dark force will be defeated by the presence of the Holy Spirit. Paul said, "I know that this will turn out for my deliverance through your prayer and the supply of the Spirit of Jesus Christ" (Philippians 1.19). The Holy Spirit is on site in the life of believers and regularly flows in their lives.

THE OUTFLOWING OF THE HOLY SPIRIT

The outflowing of the Spirit is the outward working of the Holy Spirit from the believer's life. One must have the indwelling of the Spirit before having the outflow of the Spirit.

The indwelling Spirit of God wants to flow out of a believer like the stream of a river. Jesus said, "Whoever believes in me, as Scripture has said, rivers of living water will flow from within them" (John 3:37). Jesus presented the outflow of the Holy Spirit as the stream of a river. A stream is a flowing river. It is not a stagnant body of water. It is a river that flows to where it wishes. Jesus said that a river of the Holy Spirit flows from within the believer. A believer has the indwelling of the Spirit from the moment of being born-again.

Subsequently, the believer has an outflow of the indwelling Spirit. The Holy Spirit does not want to be limited to the life of a believer. He wants to flow out from the life of a believer into the world around him. A believer's life will be more powerful when the Holy Spirit flows through him. The Holy Spirit has the first impact upon the believer himself as a river would do upon its banks. A river turns the dry places into a lush green garden. For example, most of the green areas we can find in Egypt today is along the Nile river. Many major economic activities take place along the Nile because of its benefit. As a saying goes, "No Nile, No Egypt." If the Nile does not flow, there will be no food or water in Egypt. The impact of the Nile has been significant throughout the history of Egypt.

The impact of the Holy Spirit can also be just as significant when he freely flows in and out through the life of the believer. Jesus emphasized the need for the outflow of the Spirit when he told his disciples that they would be baptized with the Holy Spirit (Acts 1:5). Jesus himself was baptized with the Holy Spirit as well as water when the Holy Spirit came upon him in a form of a dove (Luke 3:21). Jesus did not need to be born-again from the Spirit because he was already conceived by the Holy Spirit (Luke 1:35). But Jesus still needed to be baptized with the

Holy Spirit. Jesus was the first New Testament figure to be baptized with the Holy Spirit. As soon as he received the baptism in the Holy Spirit, he entered into the realm of the Spirit. Heaven was opened and the audible voice of the Father spoke to him (Luke 3:22). Jesus was immediately led to the wilderness by the Spirit after he was baptized. Jesus did not encounter the devil in the wilderness before he was baptized and empowered by the Holy Spirit (Matthew 4:1). Jesus did not start his ministry until being baptized with the Holy Spirit.

After that he began his teaching, preaching and healing ministry. Jesus said, "the Spirit of the Lord is on me, because he has anointed me to proclaim good news to the poor. He has sent me to proclaim freedom for the prisoners and recovery of sight for the blind, to set the oppressed free, to proclaim the year of the Lord's favor" (Luke 4:18-19). The baptism in the Holy Spirit empowered Jesus with power. In similar fashion, baptism with the Holy Spirit gives believers powerful experiences with the Holy Spirit. Believers will be open to the full extent of the realm of the Spirit after getting baptized with the Holy Spirit.

Baptism in the Holy Spirit gives us a greater opportunity to discover spiritual reality. Baptism in the Holy Spirit educes the life and ministry of believers with the fire of the Holy Spirit. Jesus told his disciples that they would be clothed with the fire of the Holy Spirit (Luke 24:49). The fire of God overwhelmed them the moment they were baptized with the Holy Spirit on the day of Pentecost (Acts 2:3).

Clothing is something a person wears to cover oneself externally. It is visible to everyone. When the fire of the Holy Spirit clothes us, everybody around us will witness the fire upon us. When the fire of the Holy Spirit came upon a bush, Moses could see the burning bush from a distance (Exodus 3:2). The Holy Spirit baptized life is a life of fire.

Jesus instructed his disciples to wait in Jerusalem (not doing anything) until they should get baptized with the Holy Spirit (Acts 1:4-5). He instructed them to first get baptism with the Holy Spirit to get completely submerged into the fire of Holy Spirit. Not much was going on with the disciples until the day of Pentecost arrived. Their Christian lives and ministry were not impactful. They were cold Christians!

The disciples were baptized with the Holy Spirit on the day of Pentecost. They were clothed with the mighty outpouring of the Holy Spirit (Acts 2:4). They looked drunk. Some people made fun of them and said, "They have had too much wine. "Then Peter stood up with the eleven, raised his voice and addressed the crowd: "Fellow Jews and all of you who live in Jerusalem, let me explain this to you; listen carefully to what I say. These people are not drunk, as you suppose. It's only nine in the morning!" (Acts 2:14-15).

Obviously, to get drunk, one must drink a lot. They had a lot of the Holy Spirit which made them act drunk as pointed out by many around them. Being drunk is not a private matter. A drunk person is easily be recognized by others. A person who is baptized with the Holy Spirit can easily be noticed. "Baptism in the Holy Spirit" is Biblical language even though Pentecostal and Charismatic groups are commonly associated with such a practice. Even though Pentecostals and Charismatics are known to believe in baptism in the Holy Spirit. Nevertheless, it is not well understood. Baptism in the Holy Spirit is biblical. The Bible tells us that God will pour out his Spirit upon all people (Acts 2:17). It does not say that only a few selected groups or denominations will receive him. The blessing of the baptism in the Holy Spirit is for all who eagerly desire it. On the day of Pentecost, Peter addressed a crowd of people from different cultures and languages saying "you will receive the gift of the Holy Spirit. The promise is for you and your children and for all who are far off—for all whom the Lord our God will call" (Acts 2:38-39).

The disciples acted in the open realm of the Spirit after the Holy Spirit came upon them. To be baptized with the Holy Spirit is to be submerged into the realm of the Spirit. A person who is baptized with the Holy

Spirit has greater opportunities to receive visions, dreams and revelations from the Lord. Peter declared that the outpouring of the Spirit is on all people. They will prophesy, see visions, and dream dreams (Acts 2:17). The disciples fully came under the realm of the Spirit on the day of Pentecost. To be baptized with the Holy Spirit is to fully come under the realm of the Spirit. The disciples acted under the realm of the Spirit throughout the Book of Acts. They proclaimed the Word of God in the realm of the Spirit. They preached about Christ and his kingdom in the realm of the Spirit. They healed the sick under the realm of the Spirit. They resisted opposition from the highest level in the realm of the Spirit. They raised the dead in the realm of the Spirit. They cast out demons in the realm of the Spirit. They received dreams, visions and revelations in the realm of the Spirit. They regularly fasted and prayed in the realm of the Spirit. They performed mighty miracles in the realm of the Spirit. The Book of Acts is the disciples' action under the realm of the Spirit.

The Baptism with the Holy Spirit opens us up to a deeper realm of the Spirit. Being baptized with the Spirit gives us deeper experience in the realm of the Spirit. The realm of the Spirit dominates us if we get baptized or totally immersed in the Holy Spirit. Jesus first breathed the Holy Spirit on his disciples (John 20:22). Because that was not enough, he told them to wait until they will be clothed with the power of the Holy Spirit (Luke 24:49). We need to be dominated by the Holy Spirit to live in the realm of the Holy Spirit. If we live in the realm of the Spirit, our decisions come from the Spirit. We must first relate to the Spirit before we live in the realm of the Spirit. We have to first become the temple for the Spirit of God. Solomon first built the temple before the glory of God (2 Chronicles 7:1). We are the temple of the Holy Spirit. The Spirit must first live in us. The Spirit must first fill us. We must first have the Spirit dwell in us before helping us live in his realm. The Holy Spirit shapes our thinking and desires if he dwells in us. If the Holy Spirit does not dwell in us, our flesh directs and guides our thoughts and actions.

Jesus started his earthly ministry after he came into the realm of the Holy Spirit. In Luke 4: 18: Jesus said, "The Spirit of the Lord is on me, because he has anointed me to proclaim good news to the poor. He has sent me to proclaim freedom for the prisoners and recovery of sight for the blind, to set the oppressed free."

Jesus told His disciples to first be baptized with the Holy Spirit. He gave them this command: "Do not leave Jerusalem, but wait for the gift my Father promised, which you have heard me speak about. For John baptized with water, but in a few days you will be baptized with the Holy Spirit" (Acts 1:4).

The outflow of the Spirit engages us with the power, wisdom and knowledge of the work of the Holy Spirit. The Holy Spirit works in us in a greater way after we get baptized with the Holy Spirit. The baptism in the Holy Spirit raises our experience with the Holy Spirit to a higher level. To be baptized with the Holy Spirit is to dive into the abundant overflow of the Holy Spirit.

On the day of Pentecost, the Spirit blew like a mighty wind. The Holy Spirit establishes his realm with strong wind and fire to set up his realm. He breathes upon any object. The Holy Spirit came as an unstoppable mighty wind, mighty fire, mighty river, mighty rain and mighty cloud. Who can tell where the wind or fire may go? Who is the higher authority over the presence of the wind and fire? No one! The wind blows everything in its way. Jesus said, "The wind blows wherever it pleases. You hear its sound, but you cannot tell where it comes from or where it is going. So it is with everyone born of the Spirit" (John 3:8). Fire consumes everything in its way. It destroys human logic, cultural tradition, political thoughts, dominions of disease and demons.

When the Holy Spirit comes upon you, he will blow you to the direction he wants. He blew Jesus to the wilderness (Matthew 4). He blew Peter from Joppa to Cornelius's house. The Holy Spirit blew away Peter's cultural limitations of not associating with the gentiles. He blew Philip to the desert. The Holy Spirit blew away the fear of Moses. He blew away the fear of the apostles on the day of Pentecost. He wants to light your life with Holy Spirit fire. Jesus became the Baptizer with fire. The apostles became people on fire.

The realm of the Spirit continued to grow and expand in their lives and ministries from the time they got baptized with the Holy Spirit. They became unstoppable. Fear vanished. They became bold.

A person gets an indwelling of the Spirit once upon getting born-again. But the baptism in the Holy Spirit is a repeated occurrence. We observe that the baptism in the Holy Spirit occurred numerous times during the ministry of the apostles. The book of Acts shows us that Baptism in the Holy Spirit took place in Jerusalem, Samaria, Syria, Caesarea, and Ephesus. (Acts 2:4, 4:31, 8:17, 9:17, 10:44 and 19:6 respectively). Believers spoke in new tongues as given to them by the Holy Spirit as evidence of baptism in the Holy Spirit. However, speaking in the new tongues was an evidence of one being baptized with the Holy Spirit. Jesus said, "those who believe in me will speak in new tongues" (Mark 16:17).

However, baptism in the Holy Spirit has a much greater purpose than just having believers to speak in the new language. The Holy Spirit baptized the believers to increase their knowledge about Jesus. Jesus said, "the advocate, the Holy Spirit, whom the Father will send in my name, will teach you all things and will remind you of everything I have said to you" (John 14:17). The Holy Spirit gets an opportunity to exalt Jesus in the life of the believer when the believer gets baptized with the Holy Spirit. The Book of Act tells us that the disciples of Christ demonstrated the power of Christ more than just speaking in new tongues. However, many believers do not understand the fact that baptism with the Holy Spirit has greater purpose of revealing Jesus to them than to have an evidence of speaking in new tongues. This is to say that speaking in the new language is only an initial evidence of baptism in the Holy Spirit, not an end by itself. Many who have received baptism in the Holy Spirit could have greater experience of walking in the greater power of Christ than just speaking in new tongues.

The Bible teaches us of many ways one can get baptized with the Holy Spirit. We are baptized in different ways but the same Holy Spirit gives the baptism. To receive the baptism in the Holy Spirit, one must be prepared. Jesus said, those who wants to be baptized with the Holy Spirit must do the following. First, they must desire it. In Jesus' terms one must be thirsty for the Holy Spirit (John 7:37. Second, they need to go to him. Jesus said, said, "come to me" (John 7:37). We have to be in relationship with Jesus to receive the baptism in the Holy Spirit. John the Baptist said, Jesus will baptize you with the Holy Spirit (Matthew 3:11). However, Jesus baptizes those who accept him and follow him. Third, expect to be baptized with the Holy Spirit. Jesus told his disciples to wait until they would be baptized with the Holy Spirit. Jesus gave them this command: "Do not leave Jerusalem, but wait for the gift my Father promised, which you have heard me speak about. For John baptized with water, but in a few days, you will be baptized with the Holy Spirit" (Acts 1:4-5).

The Bible gives us different accounts of the way the disciples received it. The first time the disciples received the Holy Spirit was while they were praying. Acts 1:14 reads that they all joined together constantly in prayer before the Holy Spirit came upon them on the day of Pentecost. They also prayed before receiving the baptism in the Holy Spirit the second time in Jerusalem. Acts 4: 31 reads, "after they prayed, the place where they were meeting was shaken. And they were all filled with the Holy Spirit." We also notice that the Roman centurion named Cornelius regularly prayed for a long time to receive the baptism in the Holy Spirit during Peter's visit at his home in Caesarea (Acts 10: 2, 44). Others received the baptism in the Holy Spirit while listening to the Word of God. The household of Cornelius received baptism in the Spirit while Peter was sharing the Word of God with them. "While Peter was still speaking these words, the Holy Spirit came on all who heard the message" (Acts 10:44).

The Samaritan believers were baptized with the Holy Spirit when John and Peter prayed for them before they laid their hands on them (Acts 8:15). Saul prayed to be baptized with the Holy Spirit. The scriptures tell us, "So the Lord said to Ananias, "Arise and go to the street called Straight, and inquire at the house of Judas for one called Saul of Tarsus, for behold, he is praying. And Ananias went his way and entered the house; and laying his hands on him he said, "Brother Saul, the Lord Jesus, who appeared to you on the road as you came, has sent me that you may receive your sight and be filled with the Holy Spirit" (Acts 9:11-17).

Others received the baptism in the Holy Spirit when the Spirit-filled servants of God laid their hands on them. For example, believers in Samaria received baptism in the Holy Spirit when the Apostles Peter and John laid their hands on them, and they received the Holy Spirit (Acts 8:14-17). The Apostle Paul received the baptism in the Holy Spirit because a disciple named Ananias placed his hand on him to receive baptism in the Holy Spirit. Acts 9:17 says,

"Ananias went to the house and entered it. Placing his hand on Saul, he said, "Brother Saul, the Lord Jesus, who appeared to you on the road as you were coming here—has sent me so that you may see again and be filled with the Holy Spirit." Believers in Ephesus also received Baptism in the Holy Spirit when the Apostle Paul placed his hands on them (Acts 19:6).

I received baptism in the Holy Spirit when a man of God laid his hand on me. I was overcome by the Holy Spirit and I do not know how long I was submerged in the power of the Holy Spirit. I was completely clothed by the Holy Spirit. The Holy Spirit brings power into our lives. He is dynamite, full of power. Every time it explodes it releases power. Its power destroys everything where it is detonated. Jesus said, you will receive power when the Holy Spirit comes upon you. The power of the Holy Spirit destroys other opposing powers in a born-again believer's life.

I have also witnessed many individuals receive the Baptism in the Holy Spirit during their private prayer time. For example, my wife, Dr. Mulu Hailu. got baptized with the Holy Spirit while seeking it during her personal prayer time in her bedroom. Some others have received the baptism with the Holy Spirit while attending a meeting of Spirit-filled believers or in a Pentecostal congregation.

WAYS TO ACCESS THE REALM OF THE SPIRIT

Born-again believes have access to the realm of the Spirit. The most important step one must take to experience the realm of the Spirit is to be born-again. The indwelling Spirit of God establishes the realm of the spirit inside every born-again believer. One cannot have the realm of the Spirit without having the indwelling of the Spirit. Unless the Holy Spirit dwells inside a person, the person will not experience the realm of the Spirit in his/her life.

The Holy Spirit cannot extend his realm inside unsaved person. Such a person is born in a sinful flesh. Jesus said, "flesh gives birth to flesh" (John 3:6). Jesus was referring to the natural birth experience which occurs when a person is born from his biological parents

Needless to say, a person born of the flesh is under the control and influence of the flesh. The realm of the flesh is at work in the life of the natural person. The spirit of the natural man is subject to the realm of the flesh. The flesh's acts of sin eventually cause the natural man to die.

The dead spirit of the natural man receives new birth by the Holy Spirit. Jesus said, "the Spirit gives birth to spirit" (John 3:6). This act of the Holy Spirit is known as regeneration. The spirit of the natural man becomes born-again the very moment the Holy Spirit dwells in the natural man. Jesus told Nicodemus "one must be born-again from water and the Spirit" (John 3:3-5). A born-again believer is a child of the Spirit. He is no longer a child of the flesh. A born-again believer has been transferred from death to life. He/she has transitioned from darkness into light.

A born-again believer is born from the same Holy Spirit that gave birth to Jesus. Jesus was the first person to be born of the Spirit. The angel told Mary, "The Holy Spirit will come on you, and the power of the Most High will overshadow you. So the holy one to be born will be called the Son of God" (Luke 1:35). Since Jesus was born once from the Holy Spirit, he did not need to be born-again. But all of us need to be born-again to receive the adoption into

God's sonship (Romans 8:5). We receive adoption into God's sonship when we sincerely repent our sins and allow the Holy Spirit to enter it. The moment we repent the Spirit of the Lord comes into our spirit and sets up his realm within us. Arguably, repentance gives the spirit of a born-again believer access to the realm of the Spirit.

THE WORD OF GOD GIVES US ACCESS O THE REALM OF THE SPIRIT

The Word of God gives the believer access to the realm of the Spirit. The Word of God is the passport to the realm of the Spirit. The Word of God is full of the Spirit of God. Jesus said, "The words I have spoken to you—they are full of the Spirit" (John 6:63). Jesus spent significant amount of time teaching the Word of God before he healed and delivered with the power of the Holy Spirit.

The Word of God is the source of the realm of the Spirit. When we make room for the Word of God, we make room for the realm of the Spirit! A believer opens the way for the realm of the Spirit to come into his/her life the moment he/she receives the word of God. The Spirit works alongside the Word of God. The Holy Spirit and the Word of God are teammates to bring believers to the realm of the Spirit. "While Peter was still speaking these words, the Holy Spirit came on all who heard the message" (Acts 10:44). When Ezekiel spoke the word, "the breath of God (the Holy Spirit) entered the dry bones" (Ezekiel

37:9-10). A believer must continue to feed on the word of God. Paul advised the Colossian believers to be filled with the Word of Christ (Colossian 3:16). The Spirit could not do anything until God said a Word. While Peter was speaking the Word of God, the Holy Spirit came upon them. "While Peter was still speaking these words, the Holy Spirit came on all who heard the message" (Acts 10:44).

PRAYER GIVES US ACCESS TO THE REALM OF THE SPIRIT

Prayer grants us access to the realm of the Spirit. Jesus prayed to enter the realm of the Spirit. "As he was praying, heaven was opened and the Holy Spirit descended upon him in bodily form like a dove" (Luke 3:21-22). The disciples were prayed in Jerusalem until the Holy Spirit came upon them on the Day of Pentecost. Acts 1:14 says, "they all joined together constantly in prayer." Paul prayed for fellow believers to experience the realm of the Spirit. He wrote to the Ephesian believers, "I have not stopped giving thanks for you, remembering you in my prayers. "The God of our Lord Jesus Christ, the Father of glory, may give you the Spirit of wisdom and of revelation in the knowledge of him, having the eyes of your hearts enlightened, that you may know what is the hope to which he has called you, what are the riches of his glorious inheritance in the saints, and what is the immeasurable greatness of his power toward us who believe, according to the working of his great might that he worked in Christ" (Ephesians

1:16-19). He wrote to the Colossians believers, "We continually ask God to fill you with the knowledge of his will through all the wisdom and understanding that the Spirit gives" (Colossians 1:9). Elisha prayed, "Open his eyes, Lord, so that he may see. Then the Lord opened the servant's eyes, and he looked and saw the hills full of horses and chariots of fire all around Elisha" (2 Kings 6:17).

The indwelling Spirit encourages the believer to pray. "The Spirit helps us in our weakness. We do not know what we ought to pray for, but the Spirit himself intercedes for us through wordless groans" (Romans 8:26).

The Holy Spirit initiates the life of prayer in the believer. Prayer establishes a bond between the believer and the Holy Spirit. It establishes the born-again believer in the realm of the Spirit.

THE KINGDOM OF GOD GIVES US ACCESS TO THE REALM OF THE SPIRIT

In both the Old and New Testaments, the Holy Spirit was instrumental in establishing the kingdom of God on earth. In the Old Testament, the Holy Spirit arrived on earth before God established His kingdom at the garden of Eden. "The Spirit of God hovered over the waters" (Genesis 1:2). Before the kingdom of God was established on earth, the Holy Spirit formed his realm on the waters. The Holy Spirit had no greater purpose for establishing his realm on the water than to prepare an atmosphere for the kingdom of God before it arrived on earth. Therefore, the kingdom of God was established with the presence of the Holy Spirit. The Holy Spirit came to earth not just to make way for God to begin His creative work on earth. God sent His Spirit to earth to make the way for the establishment of His Kingdom on earth. After Adam lost his position in the kingdom of God, the Spirit of God came upon the Israelites, God's chosen people, to make a way for the coming of the Messiah. "Now therefore, if you will indeed obey my voice and keep my covenant, you shall be my treasured possession among all peoples, for all the earth is mine; and you shall be to me a kingdom of priests and a holy nation" (Exodus 19:5–6).

In the New Testament, the Holy Spirit prepared his servants before they proclaimed the kingdom of God. For example, John the Baptist was filled with the Holy Spirit before he began to proclaim the kingdom of God. "John will be great in the sight of the Lord. He is never to take wine or other fermented drink, and he will be filled with the Holy Spirit even before he is born" (Luke 1:15). "In those days John the Baptist came, preaching in the wilderness of Judea and saying, "Repent, for the kingdom of heaven has come near" (Matthew 3-1-2). Jesus received the Holy Spirit before he proclaimed the kingdom of God. In Matthew 3:16, the Holy Spirit came upon Jesus. After the Holy Spirit came upon him, Jesus began to proclaim the kingdom of God (Matthew 4:23). Jesus operated in the kingdom of God with the power of the Holy Spirit.

The Holy Spirit brought his realm upon Jesus before he took up his mandate of establishing the kingdom of God. Jesus united with the Holy Spirit to fulfil his kingdom mandate. Jesus received the Holy Spirit before proclaiming the kingdom of God. Jesus had no greater purpose than to reestablish the Kingdom of God. Jesus instructed his disciples to wait until receiving the Holy Spirit before proclaiming the kingdom of God. Then they gathered around him and asked him, "Lord, are you at this time going to restore the kingdom to Israel?" He said to them: "It is not for you to know the times or dates the Father has set by his own authority. But you will receive power when the Holy Spirit comes on you; and you will be my witnesses in Jerusalem, and in all Judea and Samaria, and to the ends of the earth" (Acts 1:6-8).

The Kingdom of God gives us access to the realm of the Spirit. The Kingdom of God is God's realm on earth. We can enter the realm of the Spirit here on earth by entering the kingdom of God.. Entering it means entering the realm of the Spirit. When we enter it, we enter the realm of the Spirit. To enter the kingdom of God is to enter the Spirit's realm of righteousness, peace and joy (Romans 14:17). The first thing Jesus insisted on was for everybody to repent and enter the kingdom of God (Mark 1:15). Jesus taught to first seek the kingdom of God (Matthew 6:33). Jesus told Nicodemus that he should be born again to see the kingdom of God. He further explained that one must be born of the Spirit and water. The kingdom of God is the realm of the Spirit. Before God established His kingdom on earth, the Holy Spirit established his realm on it.

MOVING IN THE REALM OF THE SPIRIT

In the New Testament, the Holy Spirit mainly extended his realm to believers and their belongings. Jesus came into the realm of the Spirit when the Holy Spirit came upon him. He declared, "the Spirit of the Lord is upon me because he has anointed me" (Luke 4:18). Jesus moved in the realm of the Spirit from that day onward. Therefore, he conducted his teaching, preaching and healing ministry within the powerful realm of the Spirit.

The disciples acted in the realm of the Spirit after the Holy Spirit came upon them on the day of Pentecost. The realm of the Spirit came upon them not simply for a temporary mission but dwelled in them until they completed their mission on earth. The disciples acted in the realm of the Spirit throughout the Book of Acts. They had no fear of men or demons or persecutions after the Holy Spirit used them in the realm of the spirit. There is no fear in the realm of the Spirit. "For God has not given us a spirit of fear, but of power and of love and of a sound mind" (2 Timothy 1:7). The Holy Spirit can transform our formless, empty and dark lives if we allow him to come and place our lives into His realm.

The miracles performed in the Book of Acts were performed in the realm of the Spirit. Jesus sent his disciples to serve in the realm of the Spirit. They preached, taught, cast out demons and performed miracles in the realm of the Spirit. The Book of Acts displayed them moving in the realm of the Spirit. The disciples boldly proclaimed the Name of Jesus Christ. They fasted and prayed in the realm of the Spirit. They cast out demons in the realm of the Spirit. They healed the sick in the realm of the Spirit. Paul presented his defense in the realm of the Spirit, Governor Felix feared Paul (Acts 24:25). When Stephen spoke from the scriptures while being in the realm of the Spirit, they could not stand against the wisdom the Spirit gave him as he spoke (Acts 6:10). The sorcerer could not withstand the ministry of Philip in Samaria as he presented his message of the kingdom of God within the realm of the Spirit (Acts 8:12-13). The demon possessed slave girl in the city of Philippi could not perform witchcraft because the apostle Paul moved in the city in the realm of the Spirit (Acts 16:16-19).

Even the apostles personal belongings were used as instruments in the realm of the Spirit. For example, the Apostle Paul's cloth healed sicknesses and delivered many from demons. "God did extraordinary miracles through Paul, so that even handkerchiefs and aprons that had touched him were taken to the sick, and their illnesses were cured and the evil spirits left them" (Acts 19:11-12). The Apostle Peter's shadow could heal the sick. "People brought the sick into the streets and laid them on beds and mats so that at least Peter's shadow might fall on some of them as he passed by" (Acts 5:15).

"Then Saul, who was also called Paul, filled with the Holy Spirit, looked straight at Elymas and said, "You are a child of the devil and an enemy of everything that is right! You are full of all kinds of deceit and trickery. Will you never stop perverting the right ways of the Lord? Now the hand of the Lord is against you. You are going to be blind for a time, not even able to see the light of the sun. Immediately mist and darkness came over him, and he groped about, seeking someone to lead him by the hand. When the proconsul saw what had happened, he believed, for he was amazed at the teaching about the Lord" (Acts 13:9-12). Paul said, "my message and my preaching were not with wise and persuasive words, but with a demonstration of the Spirit's power" (1 Corinthians 2:4).

Peter answered the elders in the realm of the Spirit. Then Peter, filled with the Holy Spirit, said to them: "Rulers and elders of the people! If we are being called to account today for an act of kindness shown to a man who was lame and are being asked how he was healed, then know this, you and all the people of Israel: It is by the name of Jesus Christ of Nazareth, whom you crucified but whom God raised from the dead, that this man stands before you healed" (Acts 4:8-10).

The Holy Spirit used those servants who yielded to his realm. As servants of God, all we have to do is to completely submit ourselves to him. He can only take us into his realm if we allow him to do so. The

Holy Spirit communicates with us if we position ourselves in the realm of the Spirit.

THE REALM OF THE SPIRIT IS THE REALM OF THE FATHER

The realm of the Spirit is the very presence of God the Father. The throne of the Father is in the realm of the Spirit. Isaiah saw the Father God siting on His heavenly throne in the realm of the Spirit in Heaven (Isaiah 6:1). Isaiah did not see God and His throne with his natural eyes. He saw Him in the realm of the Spirit. Isaiah said that the temple was filled with smoke (Isaiah 6:4). The smoke Isaiah saw represents the Holy Spirit. The Holy Spirit formed the realm of the Spirit around the throne of the Father. The Holy Spirit gives us access to God the Father. "We have access to the Father by one Spirit" (Ephesians 2:18). Stephen saw the glory of God in heaven the moment he was full of the Spirit (Acts 7:55). Again, Stephen also did not see the throne of God in Heaven with his physical ability but under the auspices of the Holy Spirit who created his realm around Stephen to have that experience.

God revealed Himself to Moses after the Holy Spirit established his realm upon the burning bush. Moses heard to voice of God the moment he entered the realm of the Spirit. The Holy Spirit prepared the realm of the Spirit for God the Father to communicate with Moses. Again, the Lord said to Moses that he would meet him in the realm of the Spirit when he said, "I am going to come to you in a dense cloud" (Exodus 19:9).

In the Book of Genesis, we also learn that God's voice came to the planet earth after the Holy Spirit established his realm upon the waters (Genesis 1:2-3). The Father began His creation work after the Holy Spirit established the realm of the Spirit on the water (Genesis 1:2). The voice of the Father proceeded the formation of the realm of the Spirit on earth. God began to speak to the earth's environment after the Holy Spirit formed the realm of the Spirit on earth. God created everything on earth within the realm of the Spirit. God the Father sent the Holy Spirit to earth because He knew that the Holy Spirit has the mind of the Father God to prepare the same realm He has in heaven. Therefore, the Holy Spirit set up the realm of the Spirit on earth to bring the presence of the

Father on earth. The Holy Spirit extended his realm upon the priests, prophets and kings in the Old Testament to make a way for the voice of the Father to come to them.

When we look at the account of Jesus, we notice that the Father spoke to Jesus publicly for the first time after the Holy Spirit created the realm of the Spirit upon Jesus. As Jesus was praying, heaven was opened and the Holy Spirit descended on him in bodily form like a dove. And a voice came from heaven: "You are my Son, whom I love; with you I am well pleased" (Luke 3: 21-22). Without the Holy Spirit coming upon Jesus, the voice of the Father could not have come to Jesus. The Father communicated with Jesus through the realm of the Spirit. Jesus heard the voice of God after the Holy Spirit established his realm around him.

The will of God the Father is carried out in the realm of the Spirit. God communicates His will in the realm of the Spirit. When we enter the realm of the Spirit, we align ourselves with the will of God. We understand the mind of God when we access the realm of the Spirit. God is revealed to us by his Spirit. "The Spirit searches all things, even the deep things of God. For who knows a person's thoughts except their own spirit within them? In the same way no one knows the thoughts of God except the Spirit of God" (1 Corinthians 2:10-16).

If we live with the mind of the Spirit, we live in the mind of God. We will be in right standing with Father God in the realm of the Spirit. Therefore, we have to first enter the realm of the Spirit before we can have a relationship with God. To enter the realm of the Spirit, we need to forge our relationship with the Holy Spirit. If we are in a relationship with the Spirit of God, we live in the realm of God. The Spirit positions us in the realm of God. If we live in the realm of the Spirit, we live in the realm of God the Father. The Holy Spirit keeps us in relationship with the Father. "If the Spirit dwells in us, we cry Abba, Father" (Romans 8:15).

The Spirit helps us to live in the realm of knowing God. The moment we turn on the light in our closet, we see what is in it. Similarly, the moment we enter the realm of the Spirit, we see God with His majesty and splendor. The Glory of God becomes visible when we enter the realm of the Spirit.

THE REALM OF THE SPIRIT IS THE REALM OF CHRIST

The angel told Mary that "the Holy Spirit will overshadow you" (Luke 1:35). The Holy Spirit had to overshadow the womb of Mary before she could conceive Jesus. The Holy Spirit overshadowed the womb of Mary. This means the Holy Spirit formed the realm of the Spirit over the womb of Mary. Jesus was conceived only after the Holy Spirit created his realm about the womb of Mary. "Then Mary was found to be with child from the Holy Spirit" (Matthew 1:18). Jesus could not have been incarnated had the Holy Spirit not formed the realm of the Spirit in the womb of Mary.

Jesus walked in the realm of the Spirit from the first day of his incarnation. However, Jesus began to publicly minister in the realm of the Spirit only after he was baptized in the Holy Spirit at the Jordan River (Luke 3:21). Jesus declared that, "the Spirit of the Lord is upon me, because he has anointed me." As we closely examine Jesus' ministry after being anointed, we observe that he was always in the realm of the Spirit. Jesus defeated the devil in the wilderness after he came under the realm of the Spirit (Matthew 4). Jesus gave his first sermon after he came under the realm of the Spirit (Luke 4:18). Jesus prayed frequently during his ministry on earth after he came under the realm of the Spirit (Luke 5:16, Luke 6:12). Jesus preached with authority in the realm of the Spirit (Mark 1:22). Jesus performed healings after he came under the realm of the Spirit (Luke 6:19). Jesus fasted for forty days after he came under the realm of the Spirit (Luke 4). He sent his disciples to the mission field under the realm of the Spirit. Jesus said, "Peace be with you! As the Father has sent me, I am sending you." And with that he breathed on them and said, "Receive the Holy Spirit (John 20:21-22).

The Holy Spirit leads us into the realm of Christ. "But the Advocate, the Holy Spirit, whom the Father will send in my name, will teach you all things and will remind you of everything I have said to you" (John 14:26). Stephen saw Christ standing at the right hand of the Father while he was in the Spirit.

The scripture says, "Stephen, full of the Holy Spirit, looked up to heaven and saw the glory of God, and Jesus standing at the right hand of God. "Look," he said, "I see heaven open and the Son of Man standing at the right hand of God" (Acts 7:55-56).

The Holy Spirit reveals Christ (Ephesians 3:4-5).In the book of Revelation, John said, "on the Lord's Day I was in the Spirit, and I heard behind me a loud voice like a trumpet" (Revelation 1: 10). That voice was the voice of Jesus. The Holy Spirit set up his realm for John to encounter Jesus on that day. The Holy Spirit will do the same for those who diligently want him.

The Spirit enables us to live and act in the realm of Christ. "And if anyone does not have the Spirit of Christ, they do not belong to Christ" (Romans 8:9). If we live in the realm of the Spirit, we live in the realm of Christ. The Holy Spirit introduces us into the realm of Christ. The realm of the Spirit is the mind of Christ. We act with the mind of Christ, if we enter the realm of the Spirit.

Made in the USA
Coppell, TX
11 October 2023

22691384R00059